MW01204911

DISCARD

Contemporary African Americans

DENZEL WASHINGTON

BY
ALEX SIMMONS

RSVP
**RAINTREE
STECK-VAUGHN**
P U B L I S H E R S
The Steck-Vaughn Company

Austin, Texas

Published by Raintree Steck-Vaughn, an imprint of Steck-Vaughn Company.
Produced by Mega-Books, Inc.
Design and Art Direction by Michaelis/Carpelis Design Associates.
Cover photo: Photofest

Library of Congress Cataloging-in-Publication Data
Simmons, Alex.
  Denzel Washington/by Alex Simmons.
      p. cm. — (Contemporary African Americans)
  Includes bibliographical references (p. 47) and index.
  Summary: A biography of the African-American actor who won an
Academy Award for his role in the movie *Glory*.
  ISBN 0-8172-3986-3 (Hardcover)
  ISBN 0-8172-6875-8 (Softcover)
  1. Washington, Denzel, 1954—Juvenile literature.
2. Actors—United States—Biography—Juvenile literature.
3. Afro-American actors—United States—Biography—Juvenile literature.
[1. Washington, Denzel, 1954–. 2. Actors and actresses.
3. Afro-Americans—Biography.]
I. Title. II. Series.
PN2287. W452S56 1997
791. 43' 028' 092—dc21   96-46943
[B]   CIP
                                                    AC
Printed and bound in the United States.

1 2 3 4 5 6 7 8 9 LB 00 99 98 97 96

Photo credits: ©A. Berliner/Gamma Liaison: p. 4; Ralph Dominguez/Globe Photos, Inc.: pp. 7, 13; ©Jeffrey Markowitz/Sygma: p. 8; Courtesy of Boys & Girls Clubs of America: pp. 11, 42; Courtesy of Simon & Schuster: p. 15; Focus On Sports: p. 16; ©Jon Roemer: p. 19; ©Marcel Thomas/Globe Photos, Inc.: p. 20; ©George E. Joseph: p. 22; Fred Prouser/Sipa Press: pp. 25, 33; ©Doc Pele/Stills/Retna Ltd.: p. 26; Photofest: pp. 29, 30, 34, 38; Bill Jones: p. 37; ©Fitzroy Barrett/Globe Photos, Inc.: p. 41; Sylvia Norris/Globe Photos, Inc.: p. 44.

Contents

A SUPERSTAR NIGHT

Reporters and television cameramen swarmed in the Los Angeles street, while the piercing beams of several searchlights swept across the sky. A line of stretch limousines moved slowly down the street. Just ahead of the parade of cars, a large crowd of people gathered outside a theater. This was the night of the Academy Awards, the night when the motion-picture business honored its best.

As each limousine reached the curb, an usher opened the door while fans and reporters strained to see who would exit from the car. When a tall, African-American man and his wife stepped out of a luxurious car, the crowd went into a frenzy. They had instantly recognized Denzel Washington.

Denzel Washington is considered one of the most popular African-American actors in the United States today.

Denzel flashed a warm and dazzling smile as the crowd began to cheer. Reporters fired question after question as Denzel and his wife, Pauletta, walked gracefully into the theater. Denzel looked so happy and comfortable that it was hard to tell he was nervous and a little bit worried. He had been nominated for an Oscar in the category of Best Supporting Actor for the film *Glory*.

The Oscar is a beautiful golden statue given out by the Academy of Motion Picture Arts and Sciences. The award is one of the highest honors a film actor can receive. It was important for Denzel to win that night, not just for his own career but for all African Americans who were reaching for a dream.

Inside, the theater was filled with hundreds of Hollywood's most famous actors, directors, and producers. Denzel and his wife took their seats. Many people believed that he would win this year. Denzel was not so sure. The other actors who had been nominated in his category had also done very good work. Denzel could not help thinking that it was going to be a glorious but very long night.

Soon the lights in the grand auditorium dimmed. The Hollywood crowd watched, along with millions of people from around the world, as presentations were made in many categories. At last the nominees for Best Supporting Actor were announced. When he heard the words, "The winner is Denzel Washington for the film *Glory*," Denzel experienced

Winning the Oscar for Best Supporting Actor in the film *Glory* not only added luster to Denzel's career, it also paved the way for other African-American actors.

one of the greatest moments in his life. It was an achievement and honor that he accepted on behalf of African Americans everywhere.

Years of hard work had led him to this place, this very night. He had given his best in all of his films, particularly *Glory*, but had it been enough? Tonight was not the first major turning point in Denzel Washington's life. It had not always been filled with glamour, stardom, and wealth.

As a youth Denzel had been faced with his parents' divorce, the temptations of crime, brushes with racism, and even death. He had to overcome personal and

For Denzel the road has been difficult, but the rewards have been sweet.

professional problems in order to achieve his success in life. The kid from Mount Vernon, New York, never knew as he was growing up that one day he would travel the world and meet famous people. He couldn't have known that he would become something that had not existed in America since the 1960s—an African-American film superstar. Not only is Denzel an Oscar winner, but he is also considered a romantic lead. With his recent successful movies, he is now able to draw audiences without the help of other major costars.

Denzel Washington had not known any of these things. For him the road to stardom had been long, hard, and dangerous.

SOME OF MY BEST FRIENDS

Denzel Washington was born on December 28, 1954, in Mount Vernon, New York, a small city about a half an hour north of New York City. Denzel was the middle child, with an older sister and a younger brother.

It was not easy for Denzel's parents to support three children. Mrs. Washington ran her own beauty parlor. She worked hard and had a good understanding of business. The Washington children did not see much of their father because he had three jobs. Besides his work as a minister, Reverend Washington worked for a department store and for the Mount Vernon water department. He was often gone before the children woke up and came home after they were asleep. This was hard for everyone in many ways, but it also taught Denzel that sometimes hard work was needed in order to put food on the table.

By the time he was ten years old, Denzel had his

first job. He worked in a barber shop, sweeping floors and running errands for people. Every day after school, Denzel had to make his way along Seventh Avenue and across Third Street. His path took him through the housing projects. The projects were large apartment buildings that people felt were in an area filled with crime and dangerous people. Denzel often saw the groups of boys hanging out along the street corners and in the parks. Sometimes he stopped to talk with them. After awhile he became friends with a few of them.

Still, it was the year 1964, and Denzel was very happy with his life. He went to school, had a home, a job, and good friends. Denzel recalls, however, that one of the strongest and most positive influences in his life was the Boys Club of America, now called the Boys & Girls Club of America.

The club was located in an old two-story building, and there were many different sports and games for the boys to play. Counselors at the club took the club members on camping trips. The counselors even gave them advice when any of the boys had a problem. Denzel enjoyed going to the Boys Club, and he liked many of the counselors. He especially liked one of the counselors named Mr. Charles White.

Mr. White was always telling the boys that they were important. He was very good at finding out what someone did well and then continuing to compliment that person as much as possible. Denzel strongly believes that one of the things that helped him succeed was the **positive reinforcement** he received at the Boys Club. "To do anything, you have to believe in yourself," says Denzel. "Somebody has to give you that encouragement. Charles White was always telling us, 'You can do anything you want!' That stuck!"

Denzel was a member of the club from age six until his late teens. "I was a counselor at the camp when I was 13, because I knew where everything was," he remembers. During those years, Denzel really felt as if he belonged at the club. He had fun with his friends, and things were just fine.

But things began to change in Denzel's life when busing for schoolchildren became available in Mount Vernon. Busing meant that, for the first time, parents

Denzel was ten years old when this photograph was taken of the Boys Club of Mount Vernon, New York, football team. He is in the second row, second from the left.

could send their children to schools outside their neighborhoods. The school system provided the buses needed to take the children to and from school.

Many parents believed busing helped their children get a better education. They sent them to schools that had better teachers and resources. Mr. and Mrs. Washington sent all three of their children to a school on the other side of town. This school had a largely white population.

"I was in the fifth grade," Denzel recalls. "We never ever felt scared or thought of ourselves as 'poor little black kids.'"

There were two reasons why the Washington children felt this way. One reason is that their parents had never taught them to think less of themselves. The other reason is that a lot of African-American children transferred to the school. This helped keep Denzel and his brother and sister from feeling like outsiders.

For the next three years, Denzel kept very busy. He went to school, to work, and to the Boys Club. He hung out with his friends. One friend led an amazingly unhappy life. The boy's family had gone through a number of horrible experiences, including death and prison. The boy often came over to Denzel's house to spend the night because he had nowhere else to go. Denzel says, "I remember thinking, if this guy has nothing, and he's holding it together—then I've got it good!"

Mrs. Washington also knew that some of Denzel's

Denzel's mother, pictured here with Denzel and his wife, Pauletta, was always there for Denzel, his younger brother, and his older sister while they were growing up.

friends came from very troubled families. She knew that many of Denzel's friends stayed out late, skipped school, and had very little guidance or direction. At any moment they could get into trouble, and her son would be right there with them.

This was something that Mrs. Washington knew she could not allow to happen. No matter what, she had to keep Denzel from getting into trouble.

Three

LIFE AWAY FROM HOME

Since Denzel's grades in school were good, his mother decided to enroll him in Oaklyn Academy. Oaklyn was a private school near West Point, New York. Denzel entered Oaklyn in 1968, at the age of 14. The school was filled with new faces and new views of the world.

"I remember a lot of the teachers," says Denzel. "In fact one teacher, Mr. Underwood, introduced me to reading *The New York Times*."

Denzel's teacher made reading newspapers a daily class assignment. It was a way of getting the students to learn more about what was happening around the globe. Mr. Underwood also introduced his students to many well-known authors, like F. Scott Fitzgerald and Ernest Hemingway.

Denzel's first year at Oaklyn was filled with wonders. He had never been away from home before. Now he lived at the school and only came home during holidays. School life was much different from Denzel's life back in Mount Vernon. Oaklyn Academy had more rules and structure to keep the students busy and focused.

The year 1968 was also a turning point in Denzel's life. Denzel knew his parents were having problems, but he had no idea how serious those problems were. Denzel was 14 when his parents divorced. It affected him greatly. Even today he doesn't talk about why his parents split up, but he still remembers the hurt that he and his sister and brother felt.

Life changed for Denzel after his parents' divorce. Even though Mrs. Washington owned her own

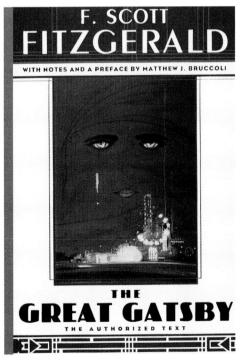

At Oaklyn Academy Denzel was influenced by Mr. Underwood, one of his teachers, who introduced him to such classics as F. Scott Fitzgerald's *The Great Gatsby*.

business, times were hard. She struggled as a single parent to provide for her children. She supported them as best she could and tried to keep them focused on their studies.

There were a number of young people growing up in Mount Vernon at the time who also had to overcome hardships. Several of them became great athletes, like Rodney McCrae, who went on to play professional basketball for the Houston Rockets.

But there were others who became trapped by the negative influences in their lives. "At least three of the guys I used to know have done time in prison," Denzel says sadly. "Anywhere from five to 15 years."

With his father gone, Denzel became a little more

Other people from Denzel's hometown of Mount Vernon, New York, were destined for fame, such as pro basketball player Rodney McCrae of the Houston Rockets.

reckless. When he came home from Oaklyn during the holidays, he started to stay out late. There were times when Mrs. Washington would go searching for Denzel and take him home. Denzel remembers the times when his mother would show up as truly embarrassing moments.

"I never did anything bad," Denzel says. "I never robbed anybody, or anything like that. But I was around people that did. I was putting myself in a position to get in trouble. It was only a matter of time before I would be in the wrong place at the wrong time."

Denzel was witness to many acts of violence. He was even asked to go along on a robbery. Wisely he chose not to take part. His own self-respect and his mother's determination had started to pay off.

"Between my brother, my sister, and me, I was the one most likely to get into trouble," Denzel recalls. "I ran with some wild people."

Denzel attended Oaklyn Academy from 1968 to 1972. "It's gone now," says Denzel. "Oaklyn was one of those schools with about 100 students."

Denzel admits that the best part of his Oaklyn days was his participation on the Oaklyn football team. "My father only came to one football game during all my high school years." It was the championship game in Denzel's senior year. Even now, almost 20 years later, the memory of that disappointment is still with him. "I remember crying and screaming at my teammates because we were getting stomped!"

Denzel's team lost the championship game, 44 to 12.

Denzel remembers those moments as if they had happened yesterday. He managed to score the only two touchdowns in the game, but he was too upset to enjoy his achievement. "My father had finally come to a game, and we lost."

Sadly Denzel's father stayed out of much of his life. Perhaps that added to the confusion he felt while he was in high school. Denzel was **competitive,** so he achieved good grades. He was second in his class when he graduated from high school. But he wasn't in love with academics. He played basketball and loved to play football, but he wasn't dreaming of a career in sports.

After graduation Denzel had no direction in mind. Even with all the advice his teachers and parents had given him, Denzel still had no idea where he was going in his life. Without direction Denzel remembers feeling lost. Despite his success in high school, he was afraid that he would wind up like some of his friends—angry, confused, and behind bars in prison. What should I do with my life, he wondered. Today he admits, "I went to college because that was what you were supposed to do."

In the fall of 1972, Denzel Washington entered Fordham University, in New York City. In his freshman year of college, he played on the football team. At first he played starting defensive back. When the head defensive coach left, however, things changed.

After a successful academic career in high school, Denzel had a difficult beginning to his college years because he wasn't sure what he wanted to do with his life.

The new coach switched Denzel to second string, which meant sitting on the bench instead of playing. Denzel remembers being faster than the starting wide receiver, yet he never got to play in a single game. For a short time, Denzel thought that this was happening because he was a freshman and that maybe freshmen were supposed to sit on the bench.

The situation puzzled him because this had never happened while he was in high school. Denzel had been a star on his old team at Oaklyn. He had always played well and hard. He never did find a reason for the coach's behavior, but he slowly realized that he was becoming frustrated and depressed.

In his sophomore year, Denzel played on the Fordham basketball team under a coach named P. J.

Carlisimo. Playing on this team did not make him feel any better. Denzel was still confused and unhappy.

Denzel wasn't any happier in his academic classes. He studied biology, political science, and journalism. Still he had no idea where he was headed. He began cutting some of his classes. Soon he felt so embarrassed about not showing up that he stopped attending classes altogether.

In 1973, at the end of the first semester of Denzel's second year of college, the school asked him not to come back. Denzel was at a low point in his life. Once again his mother came to his aid.

Mrs. Washington went down to the school with

After graduating from Fordham University in 1977, Denzel returned a few years later to receive an honorary degree.

Denzel and talked to the dean of students. In the end the dean allowed Denzel to take some time off, instead of throwing him out of school.

For six months he worked at a number of jobs. He worked at the post office and collected trash for the New York City Department of Sanitation. It did not take long for Denzel to realize that this was not what he wanted for himself. Out of all of Denzel's jobs, one job experience helped him focus his life.

During the summer he had worked as a counselor at a YMCA camp. Fellow counselors noticed Denzel had a special talent when they put on a small play for the kids. One of the camp counselors, Miles Joyce, suggested that Denzel consider a career as a performer.

Denzel returned to Fordham in the fall of 1974. He enrolled in the theater department and transferred downtown to the university's Manhattan campus. For the next two years, he worked hard on his acting and his grades. His **grade point average** went from a 1.6 to a 3.8.

"I had found my **niche**. Again it was because someone had told me, 'You're good.' We all need someone to tell us that."

Denzel's last year at Fordham helped him to realize his goals. He played the title character of Emperor Jones in the Eugene O'Neill play and the title role in William Shakespeare's play *Othello*. His performance in *Othello* gained him a lot of attention.

When Denzel graduated from Fordham in 1977, he

It was not until his senior year in college that Denzel found his true calling: acting. He is pictured here performing in a 1990 production of William Shakespeare's *Richard III*.

contracted with an agent, Otis Bigalow, who was the agent for actor Morgan Freeman. Denzel wondered what he should do next. He was out of college, and he had a goal, but he didn't know where to go from there. Was Hollywood the answer?

THE X FACTOR

"I auditioned for two TV movies. One was about Martin Luther King. The other was *Wilma,* a film about the late Olympic track star Wilma Rudolph," says Denzel.

He was offered both parts, but he took the role in the movie *Wilma.* He played Wilma Rudolph's boyfriend, who later became her husband.

On the first day of filming, Denzel met a lovely actress named Pauletta Pearson. It was Pauletta's last day on the set, so she and Denzel would not see each other until a year later. At the time they met, neither of them knew that one day they would marry and raise a family together.

In the meantime, Denzel believed he was on the right track to becoming a successful actor. But he still wasn't satisfied. One of his old Boys Club coaches, Billy Thomas, had always said that learning the basics of anything made the difference between winning and losing. Now Denzel realized that whatever he did in life, he needed to know the basics. For Denzel this meant taking acting classes to learn more about what actors need to know. He also wanted to learn about the differences between acting on a stage and in a movie or TV program.

Denzel decided to enroll in a graduate acting program. He chose the American Conservatory, in San Francisco, California. "I had seen the Conservatory's production of *The Taming of the Shrew* on PBS, and I said, 'That's where I'm going!'"

Denzel remembers leaving his mother's house with a few possessions and $800. He flew to San Francisco and checked into the Sheraton Palace Hotel, where rooms were $35 a night. Denzel knew that he could not afford to stay there for long. "By the next day, I had a $152-a-month apartment and a job at a restaurant. I knew enough to get a job at a restaurant so I could eat."

Denzel's time in San Francisco was brief. He studied at the American Conservatory for one year, then paid a short visit to Los Angeles. He returned to New York in 1978. Denzel had followed his instincts and spent extra time developing his acting skills. Now came the truly hard part of the business—the real test—could he support himself as an actor?

Not long after he returned to New York, Denzel was invited to a party. Pauletta Pearson was there. She was the actress he had met on the set of the movie

Denzel and his wife, the actress Pauletta Pearson, whom he met on the set of his first film, *Wilma*.

Wilma only a year before. Denzel was happy to see her. They began to date and realized that they enjoyed each other's company.

The rest of 1978 was filled with acting work in the theater. There was Joseph Papp's Shakespeare in the Park and numerous Off-Broadway productions. Denzel began to act in as many roles as he could, from Shakespeare to George Bernard Shaw. Denzel received acting parts in films, too. He appeared in a made-for-TV movie called *Flesh & Blood*, with Tom Berenger. And in 1981 he portrayed the son of a white businessman, played by George Segal, in the movie *Carbon Copy*.

Despite two years of theater and film work, Denzel was still miles away from making a good living. In fact, not long after he finished *Carbon Copy*, Denzel was once again standing in the unemployment line. Determined, Denzel continued performing on the stage in a number of Off-Broadway plays, including a famous African-American play by Douglas Turner Ward called *Ceremonies in Dark Old Men*.

Soon after that play closed, he was chosen to do another one called *When the Chickens Came Home to Roost*. This was Denzel's first appearance as the **charismatic** African-American leader Malcolm X. Denzel's talents were noticed, and he was soon cast in

Denzel was in the stage play *A Soldier's Play* and later was in the film version, renamed *A Soldier's Story*. He is pictured here (second from right) with the cast of the film.

The Negro **Ensemble** Company's production of *A Soldier's Play*. The Negro Ensemble Company was one of the best black professional theater groups in the United States. This was a great place for Denzel's talents to be seen.

In *A Soldier's Play*, Denzel portrayed a soldier in an all-black company of the United States Army during World War II. The black soldiers and their white commanders are stationed outside a southern town, waiting for a chance to get into the war. There is already racial tension between the townspeople and the soldiers, but when an African-American drill sergeant is murdered, accusations are made, and tempers rise. The murderer has to be found before a full-scale race riot takes place.

Denzel's performance in *A Soldier's Play* earned him a great honor in 1980. He won one of Off-Broadway's highest awards, called the Obie. The role also won Denzel the part of Dr. Phillip Chandler on a popular TV series, "St. Elsewhere," which ran from 1982 to 1988.

Denzel did not know it, but he was at the beginning of 14 years of steady work as an actor. In 1984 *A Soldier's Play* was made into a film and was then renamed *A Soldier's Story*. It starred great actors such as Howard Rollins and Adolph Caesar. Denzel was hired to recreate his role of Private Pearson, and he was praised by the critics.

From 1983 to 1990, Denzel received a lot of film work, including director Sidney Lumet's *Power* and director Richard Attenborough's *Cry Freedom*. He also received his first Oscar nomination. It was for Best Supporting Actor for his work in *Cry Freedom*.

Then came *The Mighty Quinn*, with Robert Townsend, and *Heart Condition*, with actor Bob Hoskins. Denzel was now growing as an actor because each production brought him more work and more challenges.

Something else happened during this time period. In 1983 Denzel and Pauletta were married. A year later Pauletta gave birth to their first child, John David Washington. Denzel had always felt that family was important. Now he was starting his own, right in the middle of a career on the rise. He wondered constantly if he could be a serious professional actor, a good husband, and a caring father—all at once.

In 1989 Denzel took on one of his greatest challenges. He was cast in the film *Glory*. This was based on a true story that occurred during the Civil War. It involved a company of Union soldiers, the 54th Regiment of Massachusetts. What made this regiment special was that it was made up entirely of African Americans—woodsmen, farmers, and runaway slaves. Some of them were educated men who had been born free in the northern part of the United States. Like *A Soldier's Play*, here was the tale of the African American's place in wars fought by this country.

In *Glory* Denzel portrayed a runaway slave with an unbreakable will. His work earned him the 1989

Glory was a film about an all-black company that fought in the Civil War. Denzel's performance as a runaway slave earned him the Academy Award for Best Supporting Actor in 1989.

Academy Award—the Oscar for Best Supporting Actor—his first. But this was only the beginning. For the next two years, Denzel continued to accept a wide range of roles. He was tireless in his effort to stretch himself and his skills as an actor.

Next Denzel played a jazz musician in director Spike Lee's *Mo' Better Blues* in 1990. Then in 1991 he played a cop-turned-district attorney in the film *Ricochet.* He won the NAACP Image Award for Best Actor for his role in the movie *Mississippi Masala* in 1992. The NAACP, which stands for the National Association for the Advancement of Colored People, is an organization that works to stop unfair treatment of African Americans in the United States.

Denzel worked hard to make sure that his portrayal of Malcolm X in Spike Lee's 1992 film *Malcolm X* was authentic to the last detail.

Also in 1992 Denzel once again found himself working with director Spike Lee. Denzel had come almost full circle in his career. And once again he was to play Malcolm X. This time it would be on the silver screen for millions of people to see.

Both the film and the character he played were challenges that Denzel prepared for thoroughly. He read many of Malcolm X's speeches, hired a Muslim tutor, and was even trained by Nation of Islam ministers. He knew this film was about a national hero. Many people were watching him closely to see if he would perform the role **authentically** and accurately. Denzel was determined not to let anyone down.

Chapter Five

BLUE DRESS ON MUNDY LANE

For his performance in *Malcolm X*, Denzel was nominated for an Academy Award and a Golden Globe Award. He did not win either award that year, but he did receive the Berlin Film Festival's Award for Best Actor and the NAACP Image Award.

In 1993 he went on to star in the film version of Shakespeare's *Much Ado About Nothing*, with actor-director Kenneth Branagh. In 1994 Denzel starred in the film *Philadelphia* with Tom Hanks. Here Denzel played a family man and lawyer who has to represent a gay man in an AIDS-related case. Denzel's character has to struggle with his own personal prejudices and his belief in the law and in justice.

This film was quickly followed by *The Pelican Brief*, with actress Julia Roberts. It is said that Ms. Roberts had to argue long and hard to have Denzel as her costar, since the character in John Grisham's original novel is white.

In *The Pelican Brief,* Denzel's character is an **investigative reporter** who helps a woman uncover a deadly secret. What Denzel particularly enjoyed about acting in the movie was that no matter how much danger and action was happening, Denzel's character had to remain cool, intelligent, and dedicated.

There have been a number of strong male African-American actors in films. Actors such as Laurence Fishburne, Morgan Freeman, Wesley Snipes, and Samuel L. Jackson have played many different roles. And newcomers like Will Smith and Cuba Gooding, Jr. are now building their movie careers. But few African-American men, other than the famous actor Sidney Poitier, whose career reached its peak in the 1960s, have gained the same level of status as Denzel.

For one thing Denzel is considered a romantic lead, just as Sidney Poitier was. Another reason for Denzel's status is that he has been cast as the major star in his recent pictures. This means that his picture is on the poster promoting the movie, and his name appears either before or larger than other actors in the movie credits.

Though Denzel enjoys some of the things that come with the title "star," he does not really give the name much value. He feels that the film business is difficult to predict and that one day he might not be a box-office celebrity. But he still wants people to remember and respect him for his work.

"I'm trying to be a good actor," Denzel has said.

His incredibly busy work schedule certainly has proved this to be true.

From late 1994 through mid-1995, Denzel leaped into another rapid-fire filming schedule and made three movies back-to-back. In the spring of 1994, he starred in *Crimson Tide,* with actor Gene Hackman. Then came *Virtuosity,* an action-packed summer release that pitted Denzel against a computer-generated villain. Finally there was *Devil in a Blue Dress.* This film was based on a book from a mystery series written by African-American author Walter Mosley. It was the first of Mosley's books to be made

Denzel (center) and Pauletta with Walter Mosley, who wrote the book and the screenplay for the film *Devil in a Blue Dress.*

Denzel brought to life the first African-American private eye, Easy Rawlins, in the film version of *Devil in a Blue Dress*.

into a film, and Mosley wrote the screenplay.

It was a first for Denzel, too. *Devil in a Blue Dress* was coproduced by Denzel's production company, Mundy Lane Entertainment. The name of the company came from a street on which Denzel once lived. *Devil in a Blue Dress* was the first major film his company has produced for movie theater release.

Denzel did not start Mundy Lane Entertainment just to control his own films. He wanted to do some good with his connections and position. Before *Devil in a Blue Dress*, Mundy Lane Entertainment's first project was a documentary about African-American baseball great Hank Aaron. The film was called

Chasing a Dream. It aired as a TBS cable special and received an Emmy Award nomination. Emmy Awards are similar to the Academy Award Oscars, but they are given out by the television industry.

Although Denzel had other projects in the works for Mundy Lane, there was something he had to do first—get away! In the summer of 1995, Denzel and his family boarded a plane and flew to Africa. The family planned a month of back-to-nature fun and relaxation. They traveled and camped throughout the African countries of Kenya and Tanzania, including the island of Zanzibar. They went on camera safaris and watched lions doze in the sun. They traveled across the vast range of land and were amazed by the long-necked giraffes and the powerful cape buffalo.

Africa offered many other spectacular moments for the Washington family. When they reached South Africa, they became the personal guests of President Nelson Mandela. "He took us around and showed us the prison [Robins Island] where he had been kept for 27 years," Denzel said. Although Nelson Mandela was now president of the country of South Africa, he had spent 27 years as a political prisoner in South Africa because he opposed the government's treatment of his people.

While they were in South Africa, Denzel and Pauletta renewed their wedding vows. The service was led by South Africa's highest religious leader, Archbishop Desmond Tutu. Archbishop Tutu is also famous for fighting long and hard to end the South African government's oppressive behavior.

Denzel was proud of the trip to Africa. "I had wanted this vacation to give me time with my family, and I wanted it to be educational, too." Denzel's children—John David, 12, Katia, 8, and the twins Malcolm and Olivia, 5½—received an education most children only dream about.

"I don't like to talk about my children [in interviews], because I want to protect them. But I love to talk about them because they are my children."

Denzel's enthusiasm and devotion to his children appear to have no boundaries. He bubbles and glows when he speaks about them. The same passion and conviction that make him a strong and dynamic actor are rooted in his personal life.

"My wife and I try to keep our kids grounded in reality. They spend summers with Pauletta's parents in North Carolina." Denzel smiled when he mentioned Pauletta's father. "Now there's a man someone should do a book about. He was a great educator." Although he is now retired, Mr. Pearson was the principal of a noted high school in North Carolina.

Denzel continues to speak warmly of his wife's father. "My friends call him 'the guru.' Whenever he comes to Los Angeles, they gather around to ask him questions and to listen to him speak."

Denzel believes that family ties and, in particular, his responsibilities as a father are extremely important.

Family is just as important to Denzel now as it was when he was growing up. He is pictured here with his own family, (from left) John David, Pauletta, Olivia, Malcolm, and Katia.

Maybe it has something to do with his past. Or maybe it is just his nature to give and to enjoy.

After a month in Africa, he and Pauletta went away for a few weeks on their own. Denzel returned to Hollywood and leaped into the filming of *Courage Under Fire*, with actresses Regina Taylor and Meg Ryan.

Right after completing that film, Denzel put on his producer's hat. A producer is someone who supervises or provides money for a film. His company, Mundy Lane Entertainment, had already been developing its next project, *The Preacher's Wife*, with singer-actress Whitney Houston. The film is based on the classic movie starring Cary Grant and Loretta Young called *The Bishop's Wife*.

"For me, being called a producer—that's just another title. What I did for this film [was] . . . I talked to Penny Marshall about directing it." Denzel did this after he had approached Whitney Houston to play one of the leads.

The idea of doing a remake of *The Bishop's Wife* came from Deborah Martin Chase. Ms. Chase used to

In *The Preacher's Wife*, Denzel plays an angel who helps the character played by Whitney Houston.

work for Denzel. She loved the old film and often said that it would be a perfect project for Denzel.

"We hired a couple of writers, and wrote a couple of scripts, but it just wasn't right," says Denzel. Later on, when Whitney Houston became involved, Denzel knew things were coming together. With Ms. Houston in the film, Denzel felt certain that they had a package he could take to a director.

Penny Marshall accepted the job as director. Ms. Marshall did not start out as a film director. She was once an actress best known for her role as Laverne— the sassy half of the lead characters on the TV sitcom "Laverne and Shirley." But Ms. Marshall has moved far beyond that series by directing a number of hit movies, including *A League of Their Own* and *Renaissance Man*. It was a great honor for Ms. Marshall to work with Denzel Washington and Mundy Lane Entertainment. *The Preacher's Wife* was released in the fall of 1996.

Denzel had money, awards, a beautiful wife, children he was proud of, and influence in the entertainment business. What was there left to accomplish? What could he possibly still need to do with his life?

Chapter Six

THAT'S WHO I AM

There are many things Denzel Washington still wants to accomplish. He has a strong desire to help people in need. While he was visiting his old neighborhood, a stranger once asked him when he was going to give something back to the community. The man did not know that Denzel had been doing just that for a few years now.

Not long ago Denzel and Pauletta worked hard to support The Gathering Place in South Central Los Angeles. The Gathering Place was a haven for people infected with HIV, the virus suspected of causing AIDS. The Washingtons raised funds and did all that they could, but in the end even Denzel's star status couldn't keep the shelter open.

Denzel also knows that every day that he presents himself as a hardworking African-American male, he is giving something back. Every time we see and hear of his love and devotion to his family, he is giving

For his charitable work helping others, Denzel received an honor from the city of Los Angeles.

something back. Each time we see him on the screen, portraying a different character or personality, he is giving something back.

But he has done even more. Besides supporting the haven for HIV sufferers, Denzel has donated thousands of dollars to a center for the elderly. While in South Africa, Denzel donated a million dollars to the Nelson Mandela Children's Fund. He became the national spokesperson for the Boys & Girls Club of America. Denzel becomes intense and excited when he speaks about the organization that helped keep him straight as a youth. He is especially proud of how the Boys & Girls Club has helped many people take back their communities.

"They started putting clubs in a few inner-city housing projects in Tampa and Atlanta," says Denzel. "They found out that wherever they put the clubs, crime went down 20 to 30 percent."

Even though he is a major star, Denzel Washington remains down-to-earth and is the national spokesperson for the Boys & Girls Club of America.

The study also shows that drug abuse went down in housing projects in Atlanta and Tampa, and most of the tenants began paying their rent on time. They did not want to lose their homes in a neighborhood they could be proud of.

In 1996 Denzel spoke before the United States Senate on behalf of the Boys & Girls Club. Because of Denzel's speech, and the efforts of many other people, the Senate is considering giving additional money to the organization in order to help it open more clubs in inner-city areas.

Denzel wonders how children manage to stay out of trouble today. "It must be a million times tougher for them than it was when I was young."

The thought bothered him until he remembered going to a neighborhood football game. The game was an annual event held at Crenshaw High School in South Central Los Angeles. Thousands of African-American youths gathered at the high-school stadium just to play. "There were families and friends sitting around, having fun. No fights. No craziness." Denzel's smile was bright. "I remembered thinking, this is something! Then I realized that this is going on all the time—we just don't see it!"

Denzel holds on to that memory, especially when he sees a depressing news report or hears that there is no hope for tomorrow's youth. Denzel plans to bring more positive images to the movie screen, both as a performer and as a producer. He also hopes

To Denzel, success is not measured by being a well-known actor. Success to him means being a good father and husband and a responsible member of the community.

to learn and grow more with every job he does.

"I read the Bible, and I've studied some Eastern philosophy. . . . I keep trying to see what's out there."

Denzel also wants to see his children grow up to be strong and "regular." By this Denzel means that he hopes his children will grow up to be normal people who are not too carried away by fame and fortune.

"When they visit my mother, she takes them all

over New York City. She says, 'We're going down to Harlem. And we're not rolling like your daddy. No limos. We're going to take the Number 2 bus to Lenox Avenue. Then we're going to take the train.'" This pleases Denzel and Pauletta greatly because they want their children to see more of life than just the world of Hollywood.

For Denzel Washington the future is not simply measured by how many more films he will make. Though he enjoys his success, he is reaching for something else, too. He wants to be happy. He wants to feel good about himself as a father, a husband, a human being, and a professional actor. Perhaps in that way, he is giving something back to all of us.

Important Dates

1954   Born in Mount Vernon, New York, on December 28.

1968   Enrolled at Oaklyn Academy. Parents divorce.

1972   Graduates from Oaklyn. Starts at Fordham University.

1973   Takes leave from Fordham. Works for six months.

1974   Returns to Fordham and enrolls in theater department.

1977   Graduates from Fordham. Cast in *Wilma*. Attends American Conservatory in San Francisco for one year.

1980   Cast in *When the Chickens Came Home to Roost* and in *A Soldier's Play* for The Negro Ensemble Company.

1981   Cast as Dr. Phillip Chandler in TV show "St. Elsewhere" and starred in *Carbon Copy*.

1983–
1989   Stars in *Power, A Soldier's Story, Cry Freedom, The Mighty Quinn,* and *Heart Condition*. Marries Pauletta Pearson and has first son, John David, and first daughter, Katia. Wins Academy Award for Best Supporting Actor in *Glory*.

1990   Twins Malcolm and Olivia are born. Stars in *Mo' Better Blues*.

1992   Stars in *Mississippi Masala* and *Malcolm X*.

1994–
1995   Stars in *Philadelphia, The Pelican Brief, Virtuosity, Devil in a Blue Dress,* and *Crimson Tide*. Takes trip to Africa with his family.

1996   *Courage Under Fire* and *The Preacher's Wife* released.

Glossary

authentically Done in a way that is genuine and real.

charismatic Having a special kind of leadership that inspires loyalty.

competitive Having the drive to win.

ensemble A company of actors.

grade point average The average of several grades a person receives to determine a final grade for a semester.

investigative reporter A person who gathers information for television networks or newspapers.

niche An activity particularly suited to a person.

positive reinforcement Constant encouragement for one's abilities and good behavior.

Bibliography

Lambert, Pam. "Heat from a Cool Source." *People.* July 29, 1996.

Norment, Lynn. "Denzel Washington Opens Up About Stardom, Family and Sex Appeal." *Ebony.* October 1995.

Simmons, Alex. Personal interview with Denzel Washington March 1996.

Index